Save the Pandas

THIS EDITION
Editorial Management by Oriel Square
Produced for DK by WonderLab Group LLC
Jennifer Emmett, Erica Green, Kate Hale, *Founders*

Editors Grace Hill Smith, Libby Romero, Maya Myers Michaela Weglinski;
Photography Editors Kelley Miller, Annette Kiesow, Nicole DiMella;
Managing Editor Rachel Houghton; **Designers** Project Design Company;
Researcher Michelle Harris; **Copy Editor** Lori Merritt; **Indexer** Connie Binder;
Proofreader Larry Shea; **Reading Specialist** Dr. Jennifer Albro; **Curriculum Specialist** Elaine Larson

Published in the United States by DK Publishing
1745 Broadway, 20th Floor, New York, NY 10019

Copyright © 2023 Dorling Kindersley Limited
DK, a Division of Penguin Random House LLC
23 24 25 26 10 9 8 7 6 5 4 3 2 1
001-334106-Oct/2023

A catalog record for this book
is available from the Library of Congress.
HC ISBN: 978-0-7440-7492-5
PB ISBN: 978-0-7440-7493-2

DK books are available at special discounts when purchased in bulk for sales promotions, premiums,
fundraising, or educational use. For details, contact: DK Publishing Special Markets,
1745 Broadway, 20th Floor, New York, NY 10019
SpecialSales@dk.com

Printed and bound in China

The publisher would like to thank the following for their kind permission to reproduce their images:
a=above; c=center; b=below; l=left; r=right; t=top; b/g=background

Alamy Stock Photo: Benoit Douchez / Pairi Daiza / Abacapress.com 16, Arterra Picture Library / Clement Philippe 24-25,
David Leadbitter 20bl, Cyril Ruoso / Minden Pictures 18crb, Katherine Feng / Minden Pictures 17cl, 17br,
Mitsuaki Iwago / Minden Pictures 27br, ZSSD / Minden Pictures 26bl, SCPhotos / Dallas, John Heaton 4-5;
Dreamstime.com: Galinasavina 8ca, Hungchungchih 28-29, Isselee 18bl, 30cla, Gueret Pascale 12bl, Plej92 20-21,
Slowmotiongli 8-9, Kenny Tong 18-19, Tulipmix 3; **Fotolia:** Eric Isselee 1; **Getty Images:** 500Px Plus / Fernn
Quetequitenloviajao 26-27, 30clb, China Photos / Stringer 22-23, 30bl, fStop / Sean Russell 10-11, Moment / © Philippe
Lejeanvre 14-15, Stone / Peter Adams 12-13; **naturepl.com:** Gavin Maxwell 10bl, 14bl, 30cl;
Shutterstock.com: Hung Chung Chih 26br

All other images © Dorling Kindersley
For more information see: www.dkimages.com

For the curious
www.dk.com

Save the Pandas

Ruth A. Musgrave

Contents

Meet the Panda

Wild pandas live in only one place on Earth. They live in China, in bamboo forests.

panda

Pandas are bears.
They have paws, claws,
and a short tail.

bamboo

It is cold where
pandas live.
Thick fur keeps
the bears warm.

claws

tail

The black fur might help them hide in shadows. The white fur could make the bears harder to see in the snow.

fur

paw

Scent Trail

Sniff. Rub. Scratch.
The bear sniffs the air,
the ground, and a tree.
It scratches the tree
with its claws.
That lets other bears
know it was there.

Pandas also use smells to learn about other bears nearby.

What's for Lunch?

The panda sits on the ground to eat. It holds bamboo with its paws. **Crunch**. It munches on the bamboo.

The panda uses its strong teeth and jaws to eat.

The Best Nest

The panda explores.
She looks for a den to
have her baby.
A fallen tree or rocky

nest

cave will work.
The panda makes her
nest inside.
The den will keep the
mom and baby warm.

A Baby Is Born

The new mom
holds her baby.
The mother is big.
The baby is small.

The cub is safe
and warm with her.
The baby gets milk
from its mother.

Step, step, fall.
The cub takes its
first steps.
It is shaky on its paws.
The baby quickly
learns to climb over
rocks and logs.

Soon, the growing cub races up trees, too. That is a good place to hide while its mom is busy eating.

Bamboo Bears

Pandas need bamboo forests. They cannot live without them. Most bamboo forests are gone.

People cut them down
to build roads, towns,
and farms.

Working Together

Let's save the pandas! Scientists and other people who love pandas work together. They try to learn more about these bears. They study pandas in the wild and at zoos. People are working to save bamboo forests, too.

The panda sits
in the sun.
He looks so cute!
People laugh.
Some zoo visitors
watch from just
a few feet away.
Others watch on
webcams from their
homes.
They fall in love
with the panda.
They want to
protect the bears.

The number of panda
bears is getting
bigger and bigger.
But wild pandas
still need help.
Their forests will always
need protecting.

Today, scientists know a lot about what pandas need to survive.
But they will keep learning more.

The world is coming together to save pandas and bamboo forests.

Glossary

bamboo
a kind of grass that grows into tall trees

cub
a baby bear

den
a nest built inside a log or cave

forest
a place where many trees grow and create homes for animals

scientist
a person who studies animals or other things on Earth

Index

Quiz

Answer the questions to see what you have learned. Check your answers with an adult.

1. Where do pandas live?

2. What keeps a panda warm?

3. Where do mother pandas make their dens?

4. What do baby pandas eat?

5. True or False: Only scientists can help save pandas.

1. In China, in bamboo forests 2. Fur 3. In fallen trees and rocky caves 4. Milk from their mother 5. False